Epîthalamia

WINNER OF THE 2018 AUTUMN HOUSE
CHAPBOOK CONTEST

Of the collection, contest judge Gerry LaFemina said, "Of the many things I'm wowed by in Erinn Batykefer's *Epithalamia*, what 1 appreciate most is how the poems enact a mind at work. They engage with startling language and poetic form the emotional oscillation of relationships—the combined beauty and peril that create the ecstatic state of self-transcendence. One might imagine it feels like 'Somewhere, under miles of water // a chandelier swings slowly / above the ruin of a grand staircase // its tinkling crystals silenced' because isn't that how we feel on the precipice of great love—beautiful and ruined? With their lyric prowess and meditative sensibilities, these poems are both moving and powerful the way our poetry should be."

POEMS

Epithalamia
ERINN BATYKEFER

Autumn House Press
Pittsburgh, Pennsylvania
2019

EPITHALAMIA
An Autumn House Chapbook

For information about permission to reprint, contact Autumn House Press,
5530 Penn Avenue, Pittsburgh, PA 15206.

ISBN: 978-1-938769-43-6

All Autumn House chapbooks are printed on acid-free paper and meet the
international standards of permanent books intended for purchase by libraries.

"Autumn House Press" and "Autumn House" are registered trademarks owned by Autumn House Press, a nonprofit corporation whose mission is the publication and promotion of poetry and other fine literature.

Autumn House Press receives state arts funding support through a grant from the Pennsylvania Council on the Arts, a state agency funded by the Commonwealth of Pennsylvania, and the National Endowment for the Arts, a federal agency.

WWW.AUTUMNHOUSE.ORG

CONTENTS

Epithalamia

Jane I Would Have Been

My books broke over me, too. The animals inside crawled from the pages
and stole into my skin, drawn by blood.

And I too loved a girl when I was a girl. My Helen wore her slattern-slate, her shift
like a winding sheet, and did not eat. I woke one morning

to her hand cold in my hand, her white lips parted at my ear
as if to speak. For years I heard only their silence like a sink full of water
draining and draining.

There is no Saint my Eyre can bend to in her grief, no compulsion to serve
God. Nor any god

and no heaven beyond the dark loam of the earth, its birds and fields.
She knows nothing comes afterward but the mindless parsing

of matter into other matter, heat into light. No vessel for passion
but the body, and the clay of it made to break.

The Jane I would have been is not the one who has never loved,
who does not know it when it comes, nor what deeds
it will make her capable of—

my Jane already knows
and is afraid.

Orange Peel Epithalamium

There is a car in my head.

It's medium-sized, nondescript. Beige. A sedan
of the kind Consumer Reports raves.

It's moving fast toward something or away,
and it has always been there, in my head—

the smell of my mother's skin, a hush of wind in dry grass,
summer light through leaves

and the car.

> I watch you
> page through a magazine, butter knife over toast,
> pale morning light along your cheek, your collarbone.

> I peel an orange so the rind is a long ribbon,
> and when you reach for a slice, something in me wants
> to be honest, wants

> to put a hand on your wrist and say, *let me tell you
> about the car in my head*—

There is a woman driving. She speeds along a highway lined with birches
on a wax-gray morning as if she is trying to outrun light.

She is flash eyed and thin and calm the way the walls of a dam are calm.
Something massive and brimming rolls off her in waves;

you feel them as they pass through you.
There is not one other car on the road.

> I want to tell you I am trying to stay, to eat
> the eggs you made, ignore
> the low vibration in my sternum
>
> and the car in my head as it accelerates
> through landscapes, as it glints like mica
> along a black road in the desert.

The world collapses at speeds like this. Horizon and foreground
flatten like a painting made depthless by a sheen of varnish.

The woman stares straight ahead at the horizon
where the sun will set, as if

it is a slow-closing hatch she intends to rocket through
just before it pinwheels shut.

The car is jammed with stuff. Clothes spill from bags and hampers;
a rolled-up Oriental rug juts from a rear window. A cooler
sweats on the passenger seat.

The only thing she left was an orange. She ate the meat of it, coiled
the rind into the shape of an orange and put it back in the fridge,

closed the door. Then she walked to the car in my head and got in
thinking, *Orange peel in the dark.*

> Let me tell you about the woman in the car in my head.
>
> She drives with the radio off.
> There are no sounds beyond the engine's gravelly hum
> and air drumming the windows, but it cannot drown

the sound of the refrigerator's seal sucking shut,
the sound of a key dropping to the counter with a ceramic click
like a thrown lock.

She's approaching escape velocity

as someone stumbles into the kitchen,
someone who will open the fridge and see the orange,
reach for it,

expecting an orange's heft,
and when it's crushed in his hand, she will vanish
into the white horizon.

Cold Dark Matter Epithalamium

after Cold Dark Matter: An Exploded View *by Cornelia Parker*

How to move into an unlit room? Intuition
is a stone cast from the doorway. Listen—

a ricochet says many objects. Skitter and coast says, flat
floor, far wall, no obstacle; plummet and drop says stairs.
Or no stairs.

Imagine your life as a length of white cotton string, the end
of which you cannot see, nor the beginning.

Imagine my life as a white cotton string
running parallel.

Follow them across the tabletop, into the vast expanse of woodgrain
that is the future.

What will you do if the strings do not end
but are the same string, one line rounding a corner into the other?

The space beneath my ribcage is a room in the Tate Modern,
blackout shades drawn, a bare bulb hung from the ceiling

like the meeting of spark to gas, hand to face, lips to throat.

A halo of debris moving outward. Gas can. Window frame. Spoon, spoon,
unopened letter, horseshoe.

The splintered walls of a shed, and the rupture-flung shadows a second shed.
Still exploding.

The room has two doors. One faces east, the other north,
and a wet line of patrons' prints connects them, shining white
in the bulb's shifting gleam.

Occlusion of light, of entering a corner room from different doors,
unable to see past the corona of damage.

The cast stone drops and drops, revealing nothing.

When we meet, when we touch, what will usher in?
What wreckage will we risk?

Epithalamium: Herculano

We go to the boats.

Each dark bay along the beach
is a brick-lipped mouth cut
into the cliffside,

the boats like teeth.

All day the streets shook and groaned,
and a towering stone pine rose from the mountain.

Like creatures stunned by sound after a thousand-year silence,
we went still and listened to the rain
of pumice hissing down tiled roofs.

Now we go to the boats. The muffled slap of our feet
on ash-powdered cobbles and the ragged way we gasp

the charred air through damp wool
loud in our ears.

We knew only the sweetness of honey.
We had beautiful teeth.

In two thousand years, they will gleam
up through wet black ash as a woman
with a soft brush unearths us.

Our bones will be our names:

I will be *slave,* what's left of me ridged
by fevers, starvation. Beatings
and the warping tendon-strain of labor.

The one I lie with will be *centurion* or *senator.* He was tall
and his bones sing
a litany of plenty.

The beaten metal clasp sunk in mud
at his shoulder—*fibula*—says he died
wrapped in fine boiled wool.

What our bones do not say: I did, too.

He flung his cloak around me and I breathed
through the fabric as we ran
to the boats.

But when we stumbled onto the beach the bays gaped
and howled, housed only darkness
and cut ropes.

Far out, the waves tossed mouthfuls of teeth:
all those who fled first, their boats pitching,
filling slowly with ash.

We knew no one was coming back for us.

There is nothing else to prove
what we were to each other, huddled in those bays.

The bones say he might have owned me, might have
brought a hand down hard enough
for my teeth to be knocked loose

by a sigil ring.

Or, it might have been like this: we never met
before our flight to the boats,

before death came for us on a suffocating wave of mud,
but when my eyes wept blood, he raised a hand
to my face and wiped it away.

The gold chill of his rings on my skin
was the last thing I felt.

Cataclysm is a lens, its focus
a luxury soft as ash:

who walks the cobbled sidewalk with you?

The outline of your body is a hole punched
in the August air thick as hot mud,

no different from the hollows
our vaporized remains left in the pyroclastic flow.

The ground is still. The day flawless and blue.

But if the bricks buckled beneath your feet, if the sky
rained a hail of teeth, could you
reach for him?

If your mouth gulped for air like a hooked fish,
what words would escape your lips?

To the boats. To the boats.

Epithalamium: Necrophilia

You say, *Be very still*
so I sink into a tubful of ice

and learn to breathe through my skin
like a reptile.

If I were dead, would you touch me
the way I want to be touched?

Imagine the pleated sweep of a sheet is a metal slab,
the floor a draining board,
sloped concrete the color of dirty ice.

The hose to shear away a lacquer of blood, and the hose
to draw it from me like a straw.
A soaked towel to swab me down.

I have ached for the slow ritual of stripping,
imagined you, one hand cradling my lolling head, the other
peeling the cut shirt from my shoulders.

How close my frost-rimed lips come
to your collarbone then,
but no closer.

How stark my body, the blush-siphoned skin
fish-pale and shining.

The ice cubes hiss and crack like knuckles, like teeth.
Soon, soon, they'll stop melting
against my skin

and I'll go boneless, unblinking, as if stunned
by the shock of your touch,
as if I cannot bear to look away

when you bend over me, put your lips to the cold volute
of my ear and whisper

how you want me: dead,
kin to always.

Don't move, you'll say, *Be very still.*

Maiden Voyage Epithalamium

The ocean is hungry.

A thousand-tongued mouth of black waves
licking ships,

swallowing them. They sink into a stomach
like another mouth:

the microbes miles down like teeth gnawing
ragged holes into an iron hull.

The veil falls over me like light through water.

I draw on white gloves and my hands vanish
into them.

You must believe the ocean
and its bottomless hunger

are merely scenery, something to pass
over, like a trail of blooms that leads to an altar,
a circlet of white gold.

You must embark believing
you will see shore.

How else could you begin?

The steerage-bound boy whose teeth would rake the ceiling
of his berth as he choked on icy water;

the bespoke-clad lady who would be hauled off the dance floor,
slapped silent and lowered into a life boat—

each set foot aboard what would sink,
believing it unsinkable.

The guests turn lazy circles, champagne-drunk
and leaning into one another

as the band measures a swan-song waltz
to end the night.

When your hand slides to the small of my back,
I wonder if you can feel it—

Cold stars, no moon.

The dogs loosed from their cages,
how they howl and run
the length of the ship, snapping at tongues
of rising water.

The deck beneath our box-step listing.

Inside me, a black void of freezing ocean
into which a ship could vanish.

The sea looks the same
in the morning:

flat and hungry as the turned-down bed
you lowered me into.

Somewhere, under miles of water,

a chandelier swings slowly
above the ruin of a grand staircase,

its tinkling crystals silenced
by sulfur.

Things disappear.

My body under your hands. Your body
inside me. Our bodies

into a promise vast as the cold Atlantic.

The Razor in the Apple

St. John proposes to Jane Eyre

One does not choose the shape of his ordeal.
Ringleted blonde. Olive-bearing dove,

like St. Francis she comes with exquisite kindness,
palm-up to the lowly,
the birds and dogs—

When she lays her hand on my arm to ask if we're friends,
I am a body
made of hell

and I want—

Tonight I will remember the scent I caught as she leaned in,
sweet and clean as a quartered apple,

and feel the ghost of me darkening to flesh
beneath the coverlet.

Her loveliness is the spring green of morning glory vines,
all new shoots and promise,

sinuous as temptation.

She is the fruit that falls to rot
as you bite down. And I have loved her
eyes on me, I have loved—

The thin hours past midnight are wracked with penance:
I sleep hard on the floorboards like a dog,
shoulders ribboned with lashes.

Cousin, you must know there is no overcoming the wildness
of the body, the animal pumping
of blood and breath;

no way to use it for its purpose without suffering
the horrors of pleasure.

You ask why I want you for a wife. We are alike:

I am in need of some torture by which I may prove myself,
and you wish only to be an instrument
of God before dying.

Come, let us go to a land hot as hell and teeming with devils;
our marriage bed will be made of white sheets
strewn with splintered hawthorn.

When I undress your plain, starved-small frame
I trust I shall find your body an instrument
I may mortify myself with:

your spine a flail barbed with ribs,
and no softness anywhere for comfort.

Tell me, who does not want
to be held down and made to feel
their punishment?

Who does not want
to hurt?

Parallel Universe Epithalamium

What are you now?

Once honeybee, dragonfly, red-winged blackbird, whatever I was.

And now? World without hive or nest, without the spectrum's longest wave.
Without family or phylum in which I belong.

Wherever you are, is there the myth of the hydra? A many-headed lizard
against whose necks a hero dulls his sword,

and each time a wriggling head thuds to the blood-spattered dirt, fanged mouth snapping,
two, three more spring from the wound?

The whole body splitting and branching.

Our world was one such monster.

There are moments of lucidity. Even now, wet-winged
on a flung branch—

rent leaves and cicatrized bark recall origin, taproot,
the subcutaneous beginning.

> *everything possible. everything happening. under the world's skin
> every possible world brimming—*

Wake, surface to an unraveled life: the blunt-force
trauma of dementia, car wreck, rehab; a same-body, almost life.

it is happening right now, it is happening to you right now,
happening in some other, in every other permutation, it is already happening

When lunacy draws its hand down my face like lights-out,
the last thing I think:

somewhere I am open-mouthed, somewhere your thumb
along my cheekbone, somewhere else.

I spend your lives blinking, breathing.

The shadow-selves streaming from us resonate like the lip of a ceramic bowl
ringing when the nesting bowl is lifted from it—

we inexplicably collect lake-tumbled glass in a jar, rocks pulled from a beck.

Another body we loved once swims in, walks along
those bodies of water, their other versions.

In this possibility, my world is long. In every instant of it, your worlds sheer away,
a succession of lives lived as I wake or sleep, and in each one, you die.

A year of my dreams saw lit wicks put to drapes, beams blazed and weakening.
Thunder, like a wild spring storm, and collapse.

Because once we were like bees, we are bees again,
articulations of a single organism:

the split tree grows wholly in halves, its scorched center
sending up spring-sap branches, drawing water from a deep, intact root.

Now the house is a hive of mirrors. Around every corner, not reflection
but a whole self,

divided only by space, the material of our bodies.

The bees defy physics. Their days are mundane with bilocation, a whole self parsed and occupying many spaces at once: clover, hedge, queen's quarters, air.

What separates them, the hive from the field, this world from another world? Inconsequential matter. What separates us.

Needlework Epithalamium

I am Isis of the marketplace. On every crowded street and sidewalk
of Saturday's Strip District rush

I am crouched in black river's edge-mud,
dragging the water
for pieces:

I search for your throat
among throats swathed in gauzy summer scarves,
your hands among hands that sink into
cool barrels of red lentils, yellow lentils;

the fingers weighing lychees or white eggplants
that glow like moons, lips that part
for honey-drenched tongues
of baklava.

In my net today, only wrist, wrist.
And then, your shoulder blade. Sudden,
half-hidden by ribbed cotton,

and caught one breath before the body
of the not-you it belonged to
disappeared into a sea of stalls.

This morning at a café, I collected your ankles, teeth,
and the fine arch of one rib
through the wrinkled button-down of someone

bending to help his love
into her seat before a table set with bone china, mismatched forks,
tea, and a pale slice of pear galette.

She twitched and shook, muscles
leaping like a litter of kittens knotted in a bag of skin
and tossed in the river to drown.

I left with a clicking handful of bones
and a question: could I love
as he loves, knowing from the start how it will end,

each moment spent like a coin
to cool the eyes?

As if in answer, faces rose like fish
to the roiling surface of the river:
all those I loved before I understood

loss. All those I would have chosen
not to love,
had I known.

It is like sinew-stitching scraps
of leather to make a bag
because you want to open it, because you want
to see what's inside.

I line up my tools: awl and needle. Lengths of linen
and pounded-tendon thread.

For a long time I leapt toward the fleeting bones I saw
in crowds, expecting to follow
someone's long fingers to the blue-veined crook of your elbow.

I expected your body to come
whole. Already beloved.

I know now you were butchered, scattered into a river
of other bodies

and so I am a scavenger: a raptor diving from a high wire.
I learn to glean;

I learn where to punch
through the meat of a shoulder
to stitch on its arm,

how to build a body like a house I know
but have never been inside.

To bind what falls apart
with linen.

All at once, you are assembled, bandaged in scars.

Your skin flushed faintly green as you rise
into riverlight whole.

Body I know.

Mouth I have already bitten
now speaking with a voice I've never heard.

I know how I will suffer

even as I open your shirt, press my mouth
to the notch where your collarbones almost
but do not quite meet—

Vestigial Epithalamium

The scientists say two bodies
cannot occupy the same space at once.

I know different.

Once, a shadow darkened my shadow
and another's footfalls fell
with my feet.

There was no such thing as *alone*, and then
under midwinter's seizure-white abduction light,

a nurse pressed a mask to my mouth and said, *Count back
to the beginning—*

I counted:
the warmed-over raw of Sunday steak.
Blood licked from knives and white plates.
An oyster swallowed whole.
Salt like skin.

Each number a mouthful of meat
back to the first gleaming body I ever ate.

When the anesthesia pulled thin as a latex glove
and snapped, I woke again to an emptiness
vast as my skin.

Knot of hair and eyes. Teeth like coarse white sand.
Finger bones. A second spine.
Everything scraped out of me,

shrink-wrapped in biohazard plastic
like a cheap cut of meat—

mouth sucking at an airless bag, two blue-gray pits
like a hatchling's skinned-over eyes.

Every night, I dream my abdomen is a crater
lidded in skin. Do you see?

There is no closeness close enough.
When you touch me, I feel the fraction of space between us gaping
like a great ache of salt and water.

You cup my face in your hands, run
your thumb over my lips
and flinch

at the gleaming eyeteeth unsheathed by my smile,
the empty dark inside me
that wants

to peel the skin from your shoulders
like a shirt, that wants
to be so close.

As a child I watched our butcher
fillet steaks with delicate flicks of his wrist

and wondered at the sinew-striped muscle
along his shoulders.

This was before I knew about bodies—
how badly they want to stay whole,

how intimate the strain
of unmaking.

If I crack your bones with my teeth,
you are my bones.

If I swallow
the gleaming muscle of your heart,
I feel a second pulse.

Now we'll never be alone.
You come with me
wherever I go.

Appendix A: Epithalamium

In Jane's hand; found in a jewelry box with a string of pearls.

Sighted or not, Reader, he'll not see this. After so long choosing
what is easy

over what is right, scattering coins like chicken feed to all us lowly birds
to quiet or keep us,

I can forgive him that: he is laid low now, hobbled.
I am moneyed and even.

Recall the invisible string, an artery linking the split halves of a heart
in two bodies:

when it snapped we suffered. Of course we did—
our skins bloomed bruises shaped like hands

that we'd laid on one another.
Our lips whitened, and our fingers.

But at the Whitcross branching through heath, one of us chose to walk,
and one chose to wait for winter, or for death.

It is a question of volition versus circumstance.
I chose to return.

I said, *I am your Jane and your right hand and your servant if you wish it*—
as if he could refuse. Now I say,

You look thirsty, here is water; here is my arm—let's take a turn
around the garden. And he does. He drinks; he walks.

Do you think the ring-necked dove lovely because she stays,
eats from your hand? She is only hungry.

More miraculous, the sparrow or swift, the wild gray bird in the garden
who fears you not. If you made a fist

around her as she ate, she would have chosen to be killed.
If I bear up under these pearls like an ox, I choose to.

ACKNOWLEDGMENTS

Many thanks to the publications in which these poems first appeared:

"Appendix A: Epithalamium" in *Prairie Schooner*

"Cold Dark Matter Epithalamium," "Needlework Epithalamium,"
and "Parallel Universe Epithalamium" in *Lockjaw Magazine*

"Epithalamium: Herculano" in *Connotation Press: An Online Artifact*

"Epithalamium: Necrophilia" in *Devil's Lake*

"Maiden Voyage Epithalamium," "Orange Peel Epithalamium,"
and "Vestigial Epithalamium" in *Blinders Journal*

"The Razor in the Apple" in *Blackbird*

Cage of Lit Glass by Charles Kell

Winner of the 2018 Autumn House Poetry Prize, selected by Kimiko Hahn

Not Dead Yet and Other Stories by Hadley Moore

Winner of the 2018 Autumn House Fiction Prize, selected by Dana Johnson

Limited by Body Habitus: An American Fat Story
by Jennifer Renee Blevins

Winner of the 2018 Autumn House Nonfiction Prize, selected by Daisy Hernández

Belief Is Its Own Kind of Truth, Maybe by Lori Jakiela

Epithalamia by Erinn Batykefer

Winner of the 2018 Autumn House Chapbook Prize, selected by Gerry LaFemina

Praise Song for My Children: New and Selected Poems
by Patricia Jabbeh Wesley

Heartland Calamitous by Michael Credico

Voice Message by Katherine Barrett Swett

Winner of the 2019 Donald Justice Poetry Prize, selected by Erica Dawson

The Gutter Spread Guide to Prayer by Eric Tran

Winner of the 2019 Rising Writer Prize, selected by Stacey Waite

For our full catalog please visit: autumnhouse.org